This book is dedicated to the many butterfly preserves and national parks that continue to inspire.

Copyright © 2023 by Rachel Ignotofsky

All rights reserved. Published in the United States by Crown Books for Young Readers, an imprint of Random House Children's Books, a division of Penguin Random House LLC, New York.

Crown and the colophon are registered trademarks of Penguin Random House LLC.

Visit us on the Web! rhcbooks.com

Educators and librarians, for a variety of teaching tools, visit us at RHTeachersLibrarians.com

Library of Congress Cataloging-in-Publication Data is available upon request.

ISBN 978-0-593-17657-3 (trade) | ISBN 978-0-593-17661-0 (lib. bdg.) | ISBN 978-0-593-17660-3 (ebook)

The text of this book is set in 19-point Neutraface Text Bold.

The illustrations in this book were created traditionally and using a computer.

MANUFACTURED IN CHINA

10 9 8 7 6 5 4 3 2

First Edition

RACHEL IGNOTOFSKY

WHAT'S INSIDE A CATERPILLAR COCOON?

AND OTHER QUESTIONS ABOUT MOTHS & BUTTERFLIES

CROWN BOOKS FOR YOUNG READERS
NEW YORK

Butterflies soar in the sunlight.

COLORADO HAIRSTREAK BUTTERFLY

WESTERN PYGMY BLUE BUTTERFLY

ANDAMAN CLUBTAIL BUTTERFLY

PEACOCK BUTTERFLY

DIDO LONGWING BUTTERFLY

While moths flutter
under the moon
and stars.

BELLA MOTH

SHEEP MOTH

GARDEN
TIGER MOTH

SPANISH MOON MOTH

MILIONIA MOTH

PANDORUS
SPHINX MOTH

WHITE
SATIN
MOTH

Butterflies and moths have been flying since the dinosaurs roamed the earth!

THE EXTINCT PRODRYAS PERSEPHONE BUTTERFLY

STEGOSAURUS

They are found on every continent except Antarctica.

Butterflies and moths are two different kinds of insects that are closely related.

Can you tell how they are similar?

Another way they are alike is that both start as . . .

wingless,

wiggly

caterpillars!

Their change is dramatic and mysterious.

HOW DOES THIS GROW WINGS?

Moths and butterflies have four different life stages:

1. An egg.

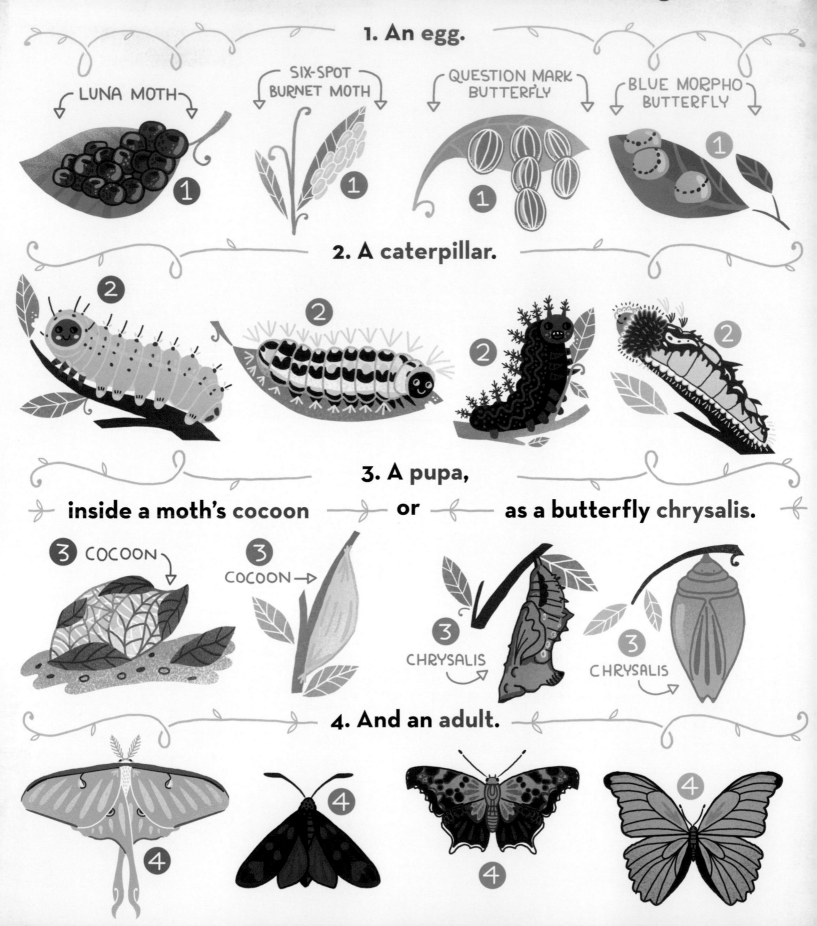

LUNA MOTH

SIX-SPOT BURNET MOTH

QUESTION MARK BUTTERFLY

BLUE MORPHO BUTTERFLY

2. A caterpillar.

3. A pupa,

inside a moth's cocoon → **or** → **as a butterfly chrysalis.**

COCOON

COCOON →

CHRYSALIS

CHRYSALIS

4. And an adult.

The transformation from egg to adult
is called metamorphosis.

Let's take a closer look, starting with an egg on a leaf.

Crunch! Munch! The baby caterpillar eats its way out of the egg.

I'M HUNGRY!

EGG

YUM!

CATERPILLAR

HOST PLANT

CATERPILLARS ARE ALSO CALLED LARVAE.

A caterpillar hatches on a host plant.

Its leaves make the perfect meal!

As the caterpillar grows, its hard skin stays the same size.

MUNCH

A STICKY SILK PAD ATTACHES.

OLD SKIN

NEW SKIN

With each growth spurt, the old skin splits and sheds away.

This is called molting.

MOST CATERPILLARS MOLT FIVE TIMES.

Some caterpillars change color when they molt!

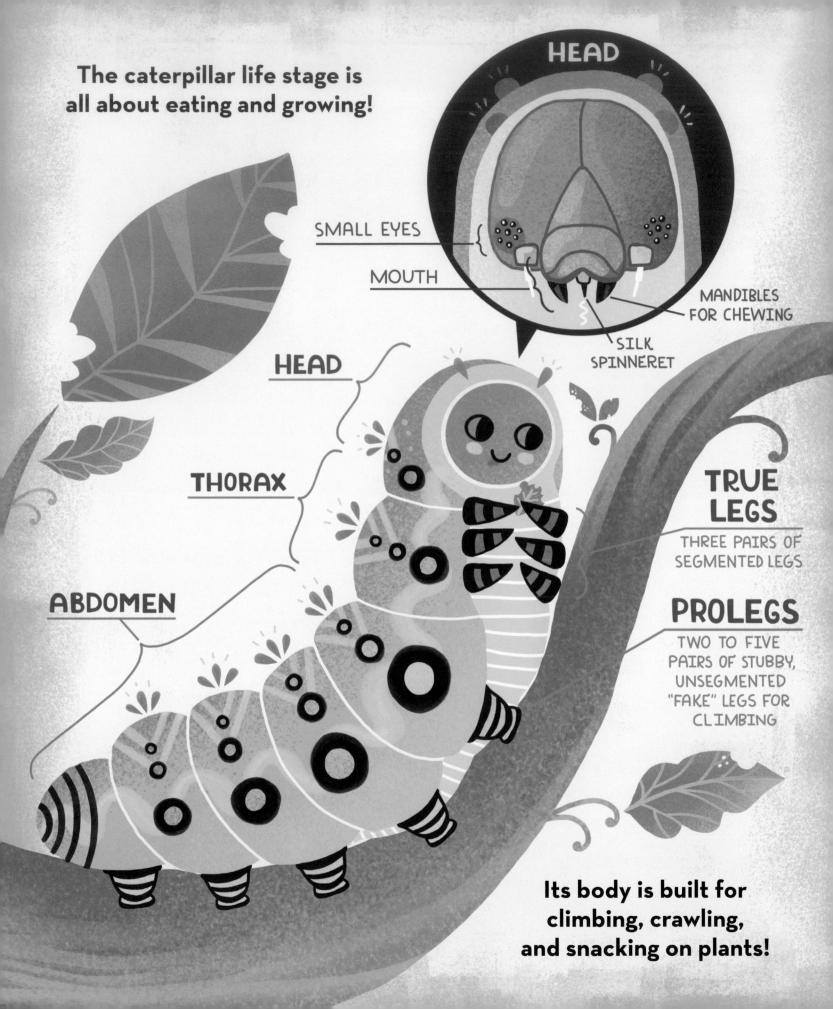

The caterpillar life stage is all about eating and growing!

HEAD

SMALL EYES

MOUTH

MANDIBLES FOR CHEWING

SILK SPINNERET

HEAD

THORAX

ABDOMEN

TRUE LEGS

THREE PAIRS OF SEGMENTED LEGS

PROLEGS

TWO TO FIVE PAIRS OF STUBBY, UNSEGMENTED "FAKE" LEGS FOR CLIMBING

Its body is built for climbing, crawling, and snacking on plants!

PUSS MOTH

THE BEAUTIFUL WOOD-NYMPH MOTH

CHAIN-DOTTED GEOMETER MOTH

ACHARIA STIMULEA MOTH

ISABELLA TIGER MOTH (THE WOOLLY BEAR)

BLACK SWALLOWTAIL BUTTERFLY

CINNABAR MOTH

SPICEBUSH SWALLOWTAIL BUTTERFLY

GRAPELEAF SKELETONIZER MOTH

Just like the butterflies and moths they will become, caterpillars can have many different shapes and sizes.

ZEBRA LONGWING BUTTERFLY

THE ROYAL WALNUT MOTH

CECROPIA MOTH

STINGING ROSE MOTH

Being a caterpillar is dangerous!

A plump caterpillar looks tasty to many other insects and animals.

YUM!

OH NO!

YUM!

YUM!

Birds, lizards, spiders, and wasps are predators, who want to make a caterpillar their lunch!

How do they survive?

Some caterpillars use camouflage to hide.

PURPLE EMPEROR MOTH

PEPPERED MOTH

BARON BUTTERFLY

BUTTERFLY CHRYSALIS

When a caterpillar grows large enough, it will molt one last time to begin its third life stage, a pupa.

A butterfly pupa is also called a chrysalis.

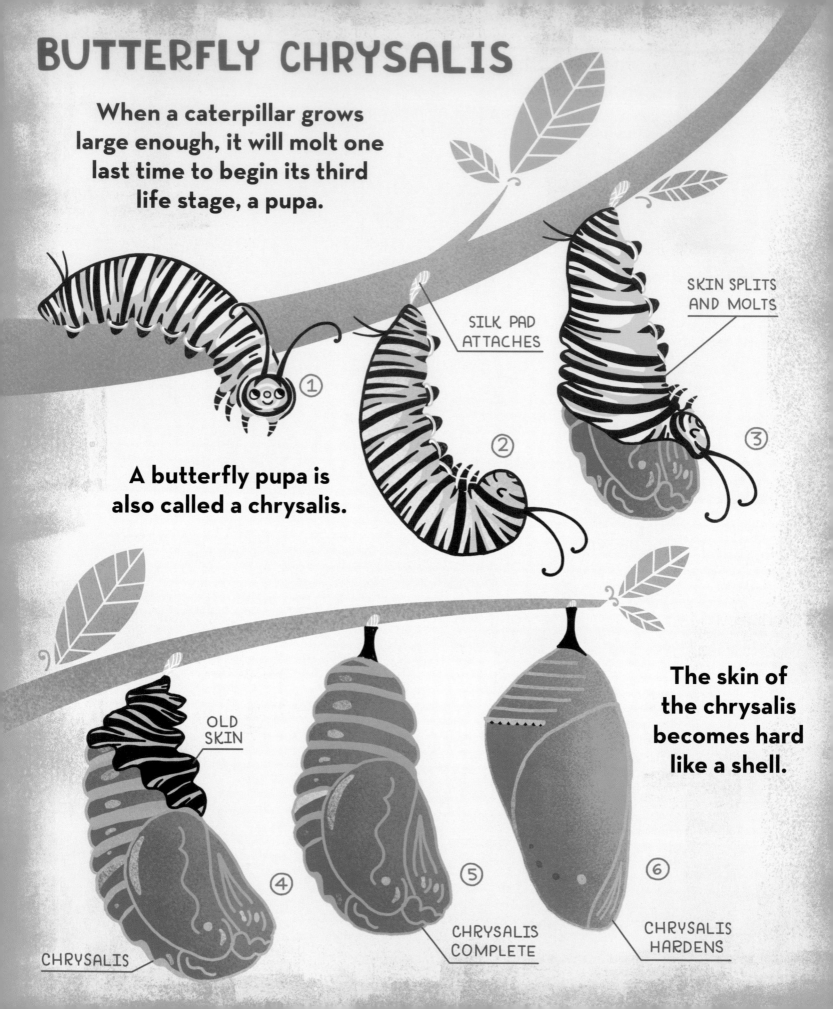

①

② SILK PAD ATTACHES

③ SKIN SPLITS AND MOLTS

The skin of the chrysalis becomes hard like a shell.

④ CHRYSALIS — OLD SKIN

⑤ CHRYSALIS COMPLETE

⑥ CHRYSALIS HARDENS

MOTH COCOON

Most moth caterpillars will spin a silk cocoon.

A cocoon is a soft pouch that will hold the delicate moth pupa.

SILK

SILK

① ② ③

④

COCOON

WHAT HAPPENS
INSIDE A COCOON

1 2 PUPA 3

CATERPILLAR

OLD SKIN MOLTS

PUPA

The moth pupa is now snuggled up safe and sound.

PUPA
LIFE STAGE SIDE BY SIDE

BUTTERFLY CHRYSALISES

← ATALA BUTTERFLY

VARIEGATED FRITILLARY BUTTERFLY →

← ZEBRA LONGWING BUTTERFLY

COMMON CROW BUTTERFLY →

MOURNING CLOAK BUTTERFLY →

← MONARCH BUTTERFLY

CLOUDED SULPHUR BUTTERFLY →

MOTH COCOONS

← BAGWORM MOTH

DOMESTIC SILK MOTH →

RHODINIA FUGAX MOTH →

POLYPHEMUS MOTH →

← FALSE BURNET MOTH

Quiet and completely still, cocoons and chrysalises come in many shapes and sizes.

SOME MOTHS BECOME A PUPA UNDERGROUND.

DEATH'S-HEAD HAWK-MOTH →

**Inside each pupa
a transformation
happens!**

**Its old body
becomes soup-like.**

**A brand-new body is created
with wings, big eyes, and
a different mouth.**

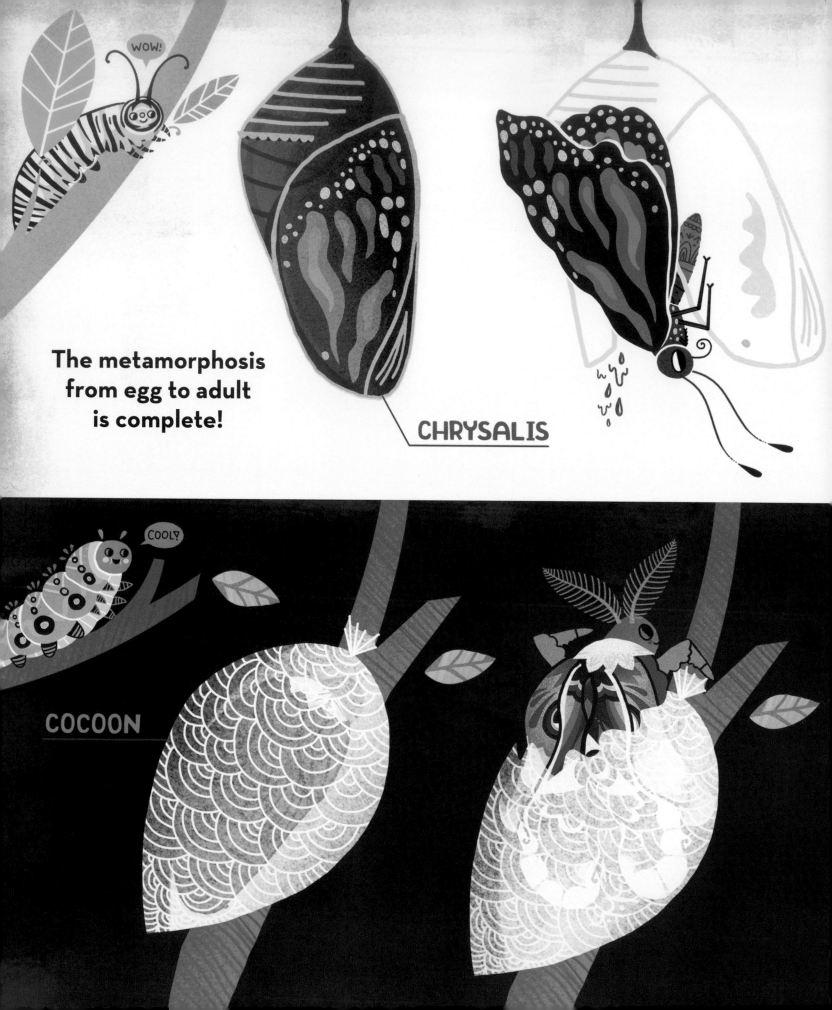

The metamorphosis from egg to adult is complete!

CHRYSALIS

COCOON

BUTTERFLY

Butterflies and moths pump
their crumpled wings until
they are sturdy and strong.

Now they are
ready to fly!

MOTH

BUTTERFLY ANATOMY

CLUBBED ANTENNAE

COMPOUND EYES

HEAD

THORAX

ABDOMEN

WINGS
FOREWING
HINDWING

THREE PAIRS OF LEGS

The final life stage of a moth and butterfly is filled with flight and beauty.

BUTTERFLIES ARE MOSTLY ACTIVE DURING THE DAY.

THEY REST WITH CLOSED WINGS.

MANY KINDS OF BUTTERFLIES HAVE BOLD COLORS.

THEIR BODIES ARE OFTEN THIN AND SMOOTH.

MOTH ANATOMY

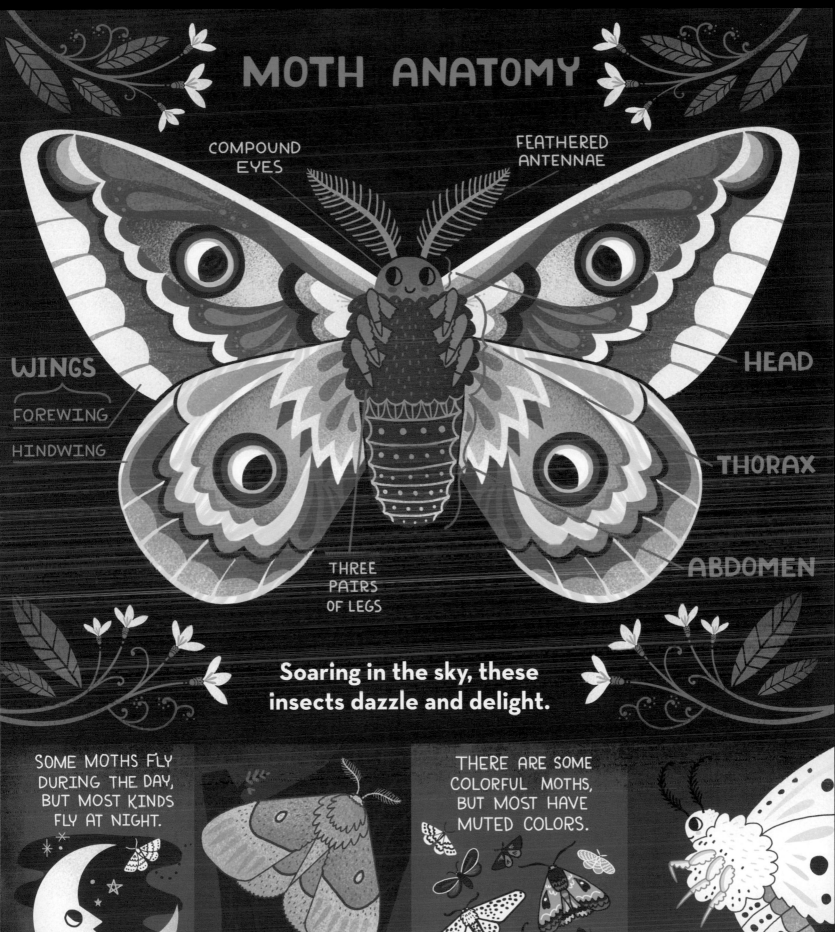

COMPOUND EYES

FEATHERED ANTENNAE

WINGS
FOREWING
HINDWING

HEAD

THORAX

ABDOMEN

THREE PAIRS OF LEGS

Soaring in the sky, these insects dazzle and delight.

SOME MOTHS FLY DURING THE DAY, BUT MOST KINDS FLY AT NIGHT.

THEY REST WITH OPEN, FOLDED WINGS.

THERE ARE SOME COLORFUL MOTHS, BUT MOST HAVE MUTED COLORS.

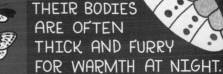

THEIR BODIES ARE OFTEN THICK AND FURRY FOR WARMTH AT NIGHT.

Butterflies and moths have teeny tiny scales all over their wings and body.

VEIN

SCALE

RHETUS DYSONII BUTTERFLY

Some have scales that shimmer and shine.

MADAGASCAN SUNSET MOTH

SALT MARSH MOTH →

Many moths have long scales that look furry.

Scales give their wings colors and patterns.
Without scales, their wings would be see-through.

ELEPHANT HAWK-MOTH

HARNESSED TIGER MOTH

FIERY ACRAEA BUTTERFLY

KAISER-I-HIND BUTTERFLY

EMERALD SWALLOWTAIL BUTTERFLY

Patterns on wings
can scare off predators
or help these insects hide.

POLYPHEMUS MOTH

DEAD LEAF BUTTERFLY

PIPEVINE SWALLOWTAIL BUTTERFLY

FALSE EYESPOTS CONFUSE PREDATORS.

COLORS WARN OF POISON.

CAMOUFLAGE!

Wings are used to flutter in gardens.
Or to travel great distances!

EVERY YEAR THOUSANDS OF MONARCH BUTTERFLIES ESCAPE WINTER BY FLYING ACROSS NORTH AMERICA.

MONARCH BUTTERFLY MIGRATION MAP

CANADA

U.S.A.

SUMMER
WINTER
SUMMER
WINTER
WINTER
SUMMER
WINTER
SUMMER

MEXICO

YOU CAN FIND THEM RESTING IN TREES.

Both butterflies and moths use sight, smell, and taste to help them navigate the world.

SIGHT
Compound eyes let them see in 360 degrees.

COMPOUND EYES ARE MADE UP OF THOUSANDS OF MINI EYES.

SMELL
Antennae "smell" from miles away.

← LUNA MOTH

They can see ultraviolet light, which is invisible to people.

← QUESTION MARK BUTTERFLY

DEATH'S-HEAD HAWK-MOTH →

TASTE
They can recognize plants by "tasting" them with their feet.

Most butterflies drink nectar from the inside of flowers.

PROBOSCIS TONGUE

EASTERN TIGER SWALLOWTAIL

POLLEN

NECTAR

Their tongue is like a long curled-up straw, perfect for reaching this sweet treat!

Certain kinds of moths can be found visiting flowers for a nighttime snack.

SILVER Y MOTH

PINK-SPOTTED HAWK-MOTH

As these insects fly to each plant, pollen sticks to their bodies . . .

CLOUDED SULPHUR BUTTERFLY

YUM! NECTAR!

POLLEN

POLLINATOR

and falls off as they drink from each flower.

POLLEN

This is how they help pollinate flowers.

Pollination is necessary for flowers to make new seeds!

CARROT

CONEFLOWER

MACADAMIA NUT TREE

Many plants depend on help from insect pollinators like butterflies.

Some butterflies will drink water in muddy puddles for minerals and salt they cannot get from flowers.

PAINTED SAWTOOTH BUTTERFLY

COMMON BLUEBOTTLE BUTTERFLY→

COMMON GRASS YELLOW BUTTERFLY→

THIS BEHAVIOR IS CALLED MUD-PUDDLING.

There are a few types of butterflies that only drink juice.

BLUE MORPHO BUTTERFLY

These butterflies snack on sap and rotting fruit.

Unlike butterflies, moths have many different eating habits.

PROBOSCIS TONGUE

HUMMINGBIRD HAWK-MOTH

There are moths that drink using their tongue, just like a butterfly.

MICROPTERIX MOTH

MANDIBLE

But there are also moths that chew and chomp on plants.

And there are moths that don't eat anything at all!

SPANISH MOON MOTH

NO WORKING MOUTHPARTS.

SHEEP MOTH

ROSY MAPLE MOTH

These moths rely only on what they ate as a caterpillar for strength.

The purpose of this final life stage is to reproduce and find a mate.

Flying far and wide, how do these little insects get each other's attention?

Most butterflies and moths rely on their antennae to smell each other from miles away.

PHEROMONES

CECROPIA MOTH →

Moths' feathered antennae are especially handy for finding each other in the dark.

ORCHARD →
SWALLOWTAIL
← BUTTERFLY

Others impress potential mates by dancing in the air.

PURPLE EMPEROR
BUTTERFLY, MALE →

← PURPLE EMPEROR
BUTTERFLY, FEMALE →

←IO MOTH, MALE

Some show
off their
shiny scales
or flash
bright colors.

IO MOTH, FEMALE →

There are even
moths that
"sing" to each
other by making
high-pitched
sounds.

←LESSER WAX
MOTH

Dancing, singing, and showing off—
all of this courtship
is to create new eggs!

After mating, each female butterfly and moth will find the perfect host plant to lay their eggs on.

EGG

GLUED TO PLANT

HOST PLANT

EUCALYPTUS GUNNII →

EASTERN TIGER SWALLOWTAIL →

COMET MOTH ♀

SUMMER LILAC →

WINECUP ↑

Each will lay hundreds of eggs!

MONARCH BUTTERFLY ↓

GRAY HAIRSTREAK BUTTERFLY

MILKWEED ↓

HYDRANGEA SPHINX MOTH ↑

HYDRANGEA ↑

From egg to adult,
metamorphosis
begins again!

Now you know
each life stage has
a special purpose.

EGG

From each egg
a baby caterpillar
will hatch.

CATERPILLAR

A caterpillar eats
and grows strong!

PUPA

The pupa
transforms
from caterpillar
to adult.

ADULT

The adult soars in the sky to find a mate and lay new eggs.

The cycle of life continues!

We have also learned how
a tiny, hungry caterpillar
can grow up to help
a garden bloom.

Through pollination,
butterflies help
flowers make
new seeds.

Certain moths help spread pollen at night.

Many wildflowers, trees, and crops depend on insect pollinators!

The forests and fields these insects depend on shrink every year.

What can we do to protect moths and butterflies?

How can we help?

Let's use what we learned and save wild spaces!

POLLINATORS WELCOMED!

BUTTERFLY GARDEN

We can grow our own gardens to help our insect friends!

We can protect nature
with knowledge
and care!

Creatures big
and small are
all important
to our planet!

SOURCES AND RESOURCES

EDUCATIONAL ACTIVITIES

Visit your local national park!
Ask a park ranger or look up what
butterflies and moths live near you.

National Park Service: nps.gov

Turn your lawn into a place for pollinators.
Look up what plants attract local butterflies.

Use the native plant finder created by
the National Wildlife Federation:
nwf.org/NativePlantFinder

Visit a natural history museum. Museums are a
great way to talk to experts, see specimens up
close, and learn more about the natural world.

For coloring pages and vocabulary
worksheets, visit the author's website:

rachelignotofskydesign.com

BOOKS

Burris, Judy, and Wayne Richards. *The Life Cycles of
Butterflies.* North Adams, MA: Storey Publishing, 2006.

Carter, David J. *Butterflies and Moths.* DK Smithsonian
Handbooks. London: DK, 2002.

Orenstein, Ronald, and Thomas Marent. *Butterflies:
Their Natural History and Diversity.* Buffalo, NY:
Firefly, 2020.